D0604097

SUPER SMART
INFORMATION
STRATEGIES

CREATING A DIGITAL PORTFOLIO

by Suzy Rabbat

CHERRY LAKE PUBLISHING • ANN ARBOR, MICHIGAN

CHERRY LAKE
Publishing

Published in the United States of America
by Cherry Lake Publishing
Ann Arbor, Michigan
www.cherrylakepublishing.com

Content Adviser: Gail Dickinson, PhD,
Associate Professor, Old Dominion University,
Norfolk, Virginia

Book design and illustration: The Design Lab

Photo credits: Page 4, ©iStockphoto.com/AVAVA; page 5, ©Blend Images/
Shutterstock, Inc.; page 11, ©Snezana Skundric/Dreamstime.com; page 21,
©Dmitriy Shironosov /Shutterstock, Inc.; page 28, ©SergiyN/Shutterstock, Inc

Library of Congress Cataloging-in-Publication Data
Rabbat, Suzy.
   Super smart information strategies : creating a digital portfolio/by Suzy
Rabbat.
   p. cm.—(Information explorer)
   Includes bibliographical references and index.
   ISBN-13: 978-1-61080-121-8 (lib. bdg.)
   ISBN-13: 978-1-61080-267-3 (pbk.)
   1. Electronic portfolios in education—Design—Juvenile literature. I.Title. II.
Series.
   LB1029.P67R33 2011   2011005580
   371.80285—dc22

Cherry Lake Publishing would like to acknowledge
the work of The Partnership for 21st Century Skills.
Please visit www.21stcenturyskills.org for more information.

Printed in the United States of America
Corporate Graphics Inc.
July 2011
CLFA09

A NOTE TO PARENTS AND TEACHERS: Please remind your children how to stay safe online before they do the activities in this book.

A NOTE TO KIDS: Always remember your safety comes first!

Table of Contents

CHAPTER ONE
What Is a Portfolio?

A portfolio helps you understand how you learn and allows you to share projects and tests you are proud of.

The word *portfolio* has come to mean different things to different people. In the business world, a portfolio is a collection of work samples organized to show a person's skills. An artist's portfolio is used to present samples of the artist's work such as sketches and paintings. For students, a learning portfolio is a collection of schoolwork.

We all feel good about our accomplishments. There's a strong sense of pride when you get a good grade on a test, solve a difficult math problem, or score the winning basket in a close game. Have you ever thought about what it takes to be successful? How do you know you've learned something new?

When you were a baby, you learned to walk and talk. As you grew, you learned how to do some things by watching others and exploring the world around you. In school, you continue to learn from your teachers and peers. What are your most successful subjects in school? Do you learn best by reading? Listening? Visualizing? Doing?

How do you learn best?

Learning is a skill we use throughout our lives. It has an impact on almost everything we do. Reflecting on your learning, or thinking about how you learn, can help you become a better learner.

A portfolio is a tool you can use to reflect on your learning. A portfolio helps tell a story of what you know and how you learn. It shows how hard you try, how much you improve, and what you accomplish. Creating a digital portfolio allows you to share your learning story with a larger audience. It can be viewed by teachers, friends, and relatives—anyone with access to a computer!

There are many different kinds of portfolios.

Excellent Work! You provided lots of details to support your answers!

READING TEST   A

In this story I can infer Sam is moving to Texas and not New York, because he told Mia he won't be needing his winter coat.

CHAPTER TWO
Reflecting on Learning

What is your favorite subject to study?

The story you tell in your digital portfolio will focus on one or more school subjects. It's up to you to decide. This requires some reflection.

Picture yourself at school. Think about the subjects you study each day. Which ones are your strongest? What makes you successful in these subjects? Perhaps it's because you find the class interesting. Maybe you don't have to work hard to do well. It could also be that you've figured out what you have to do to be successful in this subject. To get a better idea of what it means to reflect on your learning, take a look at this example.

Here's a chart that a boy named Ben used to reflect on his math class. The questions in red helped him organize his thoughts.

Subject	Think	Learn	Feel
	What do you think about as you learn new ideas in this class?	Are there any strategies that help when you are learning something new in this class?	How do you feel when you're working in class or on assignments at home?
Math	I can see patterns in numbers. Math makes sense to me.	It is easy for me to memorize facts and formulas. I can easily apply the facts and formulas to solve many kinds of problems. If I don't understand something, I ask for help and practice until I understand.	I like the challenge of solving problems. It's fun. It's like solving a puzzle or mystery. I feel successful when I can prove and explain my answers.

TRY THIS!

Create a chart like the one above. Select one of your strongest or favorite subjects, and use the questions in red to reflect on how you learn in this class.

Now, think about a subject that you find challenging. Is there one that requires more effort? Here are Ben's thoughts about that subject.

Subject	Think	Learn	Feel
	What do you think about as you learn new ideas in this class?	Are there any strategies that help when you are learning something new in this class?	How do you feel when you're working in class or on assignments at home?
Writing	I think some of the writing we do is interesting, like when we wrote about our most embarrassing moments, but I usually don't have much to say in this class.	I make sure I know all the rules of writing, like grammar rules and punctuation rules. It's a little like memorizing formulas for math. I try to think about those rules when I write, but my writing is not exciting.	I don't like writing because I have a hard time thinking of what to write. It takes me a long time to write an essay or a story, and when I'm done, my essays and stories are usually not interesting. I only write when I have an assignment. Some kids write in journals or write poetry for fun. It's not my idea of fun.

TRY THIS!

Choose a subject that you feel is important to improve. Use the same chart and think about the same questions as you reflect on this subject. Below the chart, explain why you feel it's important to improve.

You can always find a skill you can improve.

I will impruv my spelling!

Once you identify the subjects you'd like to improve, along with your strong subjects, you are ready to begin planning your portfolio.

Consider this . . .

You can design a portfolio to show only successes and how you've mastered certain skills. This is called a showcase portfolio. If you want to show how your skills have improved over time, you'll be creating a progress portfolio. You may decide to combine both ideas and create a portfolio that showcases your strengths and reflects your progress.

CHAPTER THREE
Planning Your Portfolio

Practice makes perfect when it comes to writing.

Your learning story needs three important pieces: goals, artifacts, and reflections. In Chapter 2, we worked through the steps of identifying subjects to include in the portfolio. Let's go back to Ben's example of improving writing as we explore goals, artifacts, and reflections.

Setting Goals

Many successful people set goals. They visualize what they want to achieve and create a plan to reach their goals. Some students set a goal to read all the books in a series. Others want to earn a brown belt in karate or master a difficult level of a video game. They develop a strategy or plan for achieving their goals. The plan might include carving out time to practice their skills or looking for helpful information. They may plan on asking for assistance from a friend, teacher, or parent.

Now think about a learning goal for the subject you'd like to improve. Here are two ideas to consider as you develop your portfolio:

1. **Make your goal measurable.** How will you know if you're improving and making progress? What will that look like?

2. **Have a plan.** The plan should take you from where you are to where you'd like to be. Be sure to include the steps you need to follow to reach your goal. Think of a staircase. The bottom step is where you are. The top step is your goal. All the steps in between represent the plan for reaching your goal.

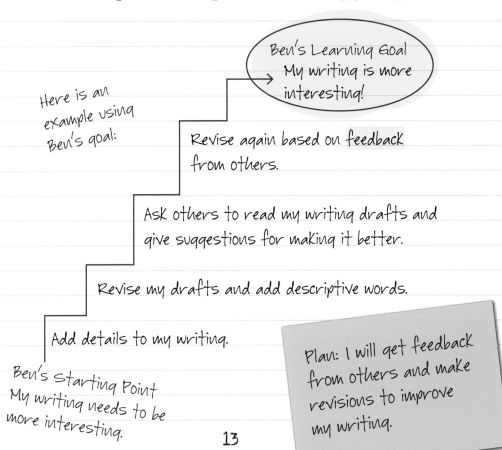

Here is an example using Ben's goal:

Ben's Learning Goal
My writing is more interesting!

Revise again based on feedback from others.

Ask others to read my writing drafts and give suggestions for making it better.

Revise my drafts and add descriptive words.

Add details to my writing.

Ben's Starting Point
My writing needs to be more interesting.

Plan: I will get feedback from others and make revisions to improve my writing.

TRY THIS!

Use the stair-step model and create your own plan for reaching your goal. Remember, the bottom step is where you are and the top step is your goal. What steps will you include along the way?

Make sure you keep your artifacts organized.

Collecting Artifacts

An artifact is a sample of your work that shows how you're doing. For example, an artifact for the writing goal can be a first draft or a revised draft. It can also be notes from a writing conference with your peers or your teacher, or a final copy of the essay. All of these documents help show the progress made toward your goal of improving your writing. It's important to date your artifacts. This will help show your progress over time.

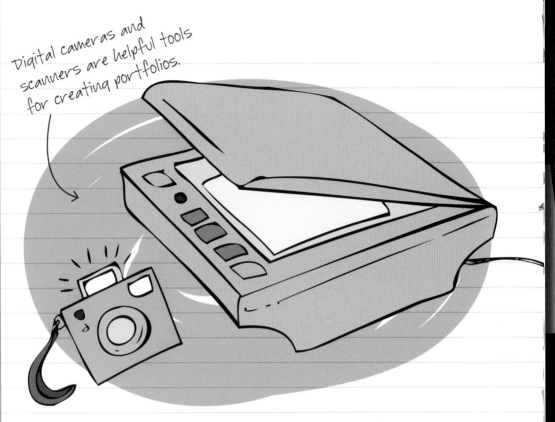

Digital cameras and scanners are helpful tools for creating portfolios.

When you create a digital portfolio, all of your artifacts will need to be converted to a digital format. This means changing pictures and documents into a format a computer can read and save. For example, if your writing draft was written by hand, it can be scanned with a document scanner and converted to a digital image or picture file.

Digital cameras are great tools you can use to capture learning. Use a digital camera to take photos of 3-dimensional models, science experiments, or the handstand you learned to do in gym! Other types of artifacts to consider are slide shows, movie files, and podcasts. There are many ways to show what you know. Be creative!

TRY THIS!

Which samples of work will you use for artifacts? How will you select them? Make a list of what you will look for in selecting artifacts. This list is like a measuring stick to help you find artifacts that show progress toward reaching your goal. It's a good idea to include your "measuring stick," or criteria, in your portfolio along with your goals.

You're sure to reach your goal if you go step-by-step.

Remember, an artifact provides evidence that shows the progress you're making toward achieving your goal in a particular subject area. If you have a great photo of your solar system model, chances are it won't be a good artifact to show how you're doing in social studies.

Reflecting on Your Progress

Self-reflection is an important part of the portfolio process. It means looking at how you would handle an assignment, test, or skill differently to gain a better understanding or earn a better grade. Use a self-reflection checklist, like the one below, to reflect on your progress as you select each artifact for your portfolio.

Here's Ben's writing checklist.

I chose this piece for my portfolio because:
- I spent time revising my writing.
- I used a thesaurus to find interesting words to add to my writing.
- I replaced some plain words such as "happy" with exciting words such as "elated."
- I asked someone to read my essay and make suggestions.
- I revised a second time.

Here's another example. Emma wants to improve her reading comprehension. She enjoys reading fiction, but sometimes has a hard time understanding her science and social studies textbooks. Her goal is to use some of the reading strategies she has learned to improve her understanding of science and social studies. Emma's artifacts may include daily assignments, quizzes, tests, and a journal where she keeps notes about her reading. When Emma received an A on her history test, she chose that as an artifact for her portfolio. Take a look at her reflection checklist.

Here's Emma's checklist. ⟶

Social Studies Report   96%
Emma

The book that I read was about the Civil War. It takes place in Mississippi. It is written from a young white boy's perspective. His family lives on a cotton plantation. His best friend is another boy who works on the farm.

I chose this piece for my portfolio because:
- I previewed the chapter before reading, looking at headings and subheadings.
- I studied the illustrations, maps, and graphs.
- I used the glossary or dictionary to find the meaning of words I didn't know.
- I tried to connect this reading to what I already know about the topic.
- I read the chapter a second time.

Emma's self-assessment checklist was created from her goal and her plan.

Although a checklist is a quick tool to use for reflection, you can also write a few sentences telling how your artifact shows evidence of your learning.

Here's one of Emma's reflections.

I chose this social studies test for my portfolio, because it shows that I understood the information in my textbook. I was able to answer the multiple-choice and the essay questions based on what I read!

Once you complete the reflection, take another look at your goal. Is it realistic—something you can accomplish? Do you need to revise your goal or change it a little to make it manageable? Have you already reached your goal? As you develop your portfolio over time, continue the cycle of selecting artifacts, reflecting, and reviewing your goal.

CHAPTER FOUR
Digital Design

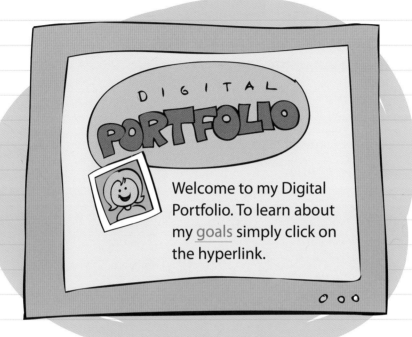

Welcome to my Digital Portfolio. To learn about my goals simply click on the hyperlink.

⌐ Hypertext stands out on a Web page.

Hypertext and Multimedia

Before you decide on a publishing tool, it's a good idea to understand the basic digital parts that make up your portfolio. We refer to the printed word on a page as text. On a Web site, you often see text that is underlined or shown in a different color. You can click on this text to link to another page or file. This is called hypertext. When you read a Web page, hypertext allows you to branch off in many directions to explore information.

The files you select for your digital portfolio are called media files. Examples of media files include digital images, electronic documents, movies, slide shows, and audio files like podcasts. Your digital portfolio can include some or all of these media files, making it a multimedia project.

Map It Out!

Every well-designed digital portfolio begins with a graphic organizer. This tool can help you develop a plan for organizing and displaying your goals, artifacts, and reflections. Start with a table of contents. It will help viewers find their way around your portfolio. Use hypertext to link your learning goals to the artifacts.

Design a well-organized portfolio so viewers can easily find what they are looking for.

From there, you can link to your reflections. Take time to develop a plan for your portfolio. It will help you visualize the best way to use hypertext to navigate through the portfolio. Here is an example:

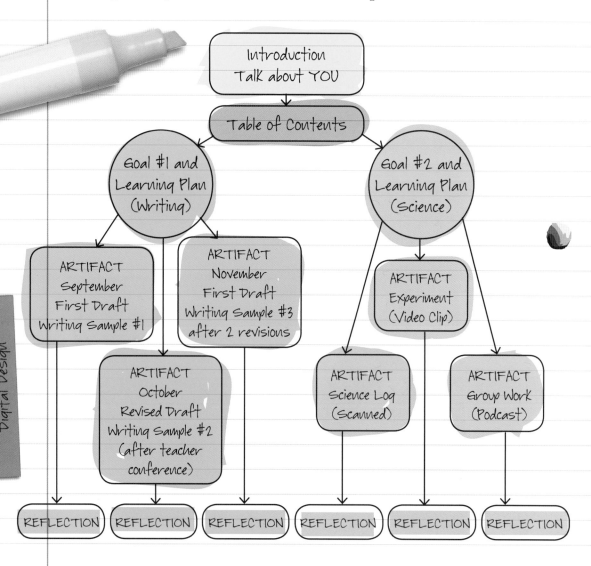

TRY THIS!

Create a graphic organizer that shows how you will organize your digital portfolio. Think about how you will link files so that people can easily navigate through your portfolio.

You will have a lot of media files to manage while working with your digital portfolio. Begin with a plan for organizing those files. First, make a folder on your computer desktop and label it Digital Portfolio. Inside this folder, create another folder for goals, one for artifacts, and a third for reflections. It's a good idea to create a fourth folder where you can store files you might use. Call that one the Working Folder.

← Creating folders will help keep your artifacts organized and make creating your portfolio easier.

CHAPTER FIVE

Publishing Your Digital Portfolio

Web 2.0 Publishing

When you visit a Web site, you can read, view, and listen to information. But Web 2.0 tools allow you to interact with the information on the Web by posting questions and adding comments. LiveBinder and Wikispaces are examples of Web 2.0 tools. Live Binder is a free online tool for storing and sharing media files like photos, videos, slide shows, PDFs and documents. You can organize your LiveBinder with Tabs to separate goals, artifacts and reflections. Teachers, family members, and friends will be able to view and comment on your portfolio entries right in your binder!

Wikispaces is another free online tool that is easy to use to showcase your portfolio. When you create a page on a wiki, a discussion page is automatically created for you. It's often marked with a special tab or link labeled "discussion." This is where you can post messages or reflections, and receive feedback from others.

Software Tools

You can also publish and store your portfolio on your computer using software. PowerPoint and Keynote are two software programs to consider for publishing your digital portfolio. You may have used these programs to create a slide show presentation. Usually you begin with a title slide and click to advance to the other slides from beginning to end. This is called a linear presentation. The slides are presented in numerical order like a straight line.

PowerPoint and Keynote also have the ability to present information in a nonlinear way using hypertext. You can insert buttons and hypertext on the slides to move from one slide to another, without traveling in a straight line.

You can use hypertext to allow viewers to see slides in any order they choose.

Let's take a look at the PowerPoint tools you can use to create buttons and hypertext. The exact steps may vary depending on the version of the program you are using.

PowerPoint Buttons

BUTTONS: To create a button, go to the toolbar and click on Slide Show. Scroll down to Action Buttons. Here you'll find some ready-made buttons with symbols and arrows to navitage through the portfolio.

PROGRAMMING THE BUTTONS: Click once on the button to select it. Go to the toolbar and click on Slide Show. Scroll down to Action Settings. Select the hyperlink option and use your map to decide where to connect this button.

As you build your digital portfolio using a stack of slides, you can insert pictures, movies, podcasts, or other audio files on your artifact slides. Reflections can be written directly on a blank slide. You may also decide to record your reflection and add that recording to the slide that displays your artifact! Here's how to add audio to your slides.

PowerPoint Audio

AUDIO: Go to the toolbar and click on Insert. Scroll down to Sound and Music, and slide your mouse to the option labeled Record Sound. A window will appear. Click on the round button to record your reflection. Click on the square button to stop when you're done. Then click on OK. The audio file will appear as a small blue speaker on your slide. Click to hear your recording.

Another presentation software program that you can use to create a digital portfolio is HyperStudio. This program allows you to create a stack of cards rather than slides. You can add all types of media files to the cards. Cards within the stack are linked with buttons. Although software tools are useful for displaying your portfolio entries, they do not provide opportunities for feedback.

Ask a parent or a teacher to help you set up an account to create a free wiki or Web site. See the Find Out More section at the back of this book for recommended sites. Create your table of contents on the first page. Add an additional page and type your goals. Link the word Goals from the Table of Contents to the page displaying your goals by creating a hyperlink. Repeat these steps for artifacts and reflections. Use your graphic organizer as a guide for organizing the pages on your site.

You can usually find directions and video tutorials on the Web site you're using to build your Web site or wiki. Follow the tutorials to learn how to upload your media files and link pages.

Designing a Web site is another option for displaying your portfolio. You will need Web authoring software like iWeb or check out the free Web authoring tool, Weebly, in the Find Out More section of this book. Add a blog to your Web site to gather feedback on your portfolio entries. The word blog stands for Web log. Adding a blog is like adding another page to the site. However, this page is designed for you to post messages like, "Check out the video of my persuasive speech!" Viewers can click on your post and add their comments. Gathering feedback from others is a great way to look at your work from a different perspective or notice something you hadn't thought of before.

Share your portfolio with family and friends.

Think about these questions as you develop your digital portfolio.

Digital Portfolio Checklist

Did you...
- identify a subject or subjects as the focus of your portfolio?
- decide on learning goals?
- develop a learning plan to help you reach those goals?
- list your criteria for selecting artifacts?
- date your artifacts?
- develop a reflection checklist?
- use a graphic organizer to plan the organization of hyperlinks and media files?
- create folders on your computer to organize your digital files?
- encourage feedback from viewers?

Your digital portfolio is your unique story of how and what you learn. Be proud to tell it and proud to share it! The outcome is up to you!

Glossary

artifacts (AHR-tuh-facts) samples of work that show what
you've learned or accomplished

criteria (krye-TEER-ee-uh) standards used to measure or
judge something

feedback (FEED-bak) written or spoken reactions to something that you have done

goals (GOHLZ) things you would like to accomplish

graphic organizer (GRAF-ik OR-guh-nye-zer) a diagram used
to organize thoughts and ideas

hypertext (HYE-pur-tekst) text that provides a link to
another area on a Web site

media (MEE-dee-uh) digital files such as images, documents,
movies, and audio recordings

peers (PEERZ) people who are the same age; classmates

portfolio (port-FOH-lee-oh) a carefully selected collection of
work that shows what you know and how you learn

progress portfolio (PRAH-gres port-FOH-lee-oh) a portfolio
designed to show how you improve over time

reflecting (ri-FLEKT-ing) thinking carefully about something

showcase portfolio (SHOH-case port-FOH-lee-oh) a portfolio
designed to show your best work

tutorials (too-TORE-ee-uhlz) papers, books, films, or computer
programs that provide instructions or information about a
particular subject

visualizing (VIZH-oo-uh-lize-ing) picturing something in your
mind

Find Out More

BOOKS

Fontichiaro, Kristin. *Podcasting 101*. Ann Arbor, MI: Cherry Lake Publishing, 2011.

Green, Julie. *Shooting Video to Make Learning Fun*. Ann Arbor, MI: Cherry Lake Publishing, 2011.

Rabbat, Suzy. *Using Digital Images*. Ann Arbor, MI: Cherry Lake Publishing, 2011.

WEB SITES

Weebly—Create a Free Web Site

www.weebly.com/

Use Weebly to publish your digital portfolio and share it with anyone who has access to the Internet.

Wikispaces

www.wikispaces.com

Design your digital portfolio with a free wiki at Wikispaces.

Index

About the Author

Suzy Rabbat is a National Board certified school librarian. She has two children, Mike and Annie. She lives in Mt. Prospect, Illinois, with her husband, Basile.